Family
Beyond
Limits

Rod Parsley

Family
Beyond
Limits

Rod Parsley

RESULTS
PUBLISHING

FAMILY BEYOND LIMITS
by Rod Parsley
Published by Results Publishing
World Harvest Church
P.O. Box 32932
Columbus, OH 43232
www.breakthrough.net

Unless otherwise noted, all Scripture notations are from the
King James Version of the Bible.

ISBN 1-933336-82-X

Printed in the United States of America.

TABLE OF CONTENTS

Chapter One
Families by the Book

God is the Author of the family, and His design...has always been a man, his wife and their children.

Chapter One
Families by the Book

At the end of a popular 1993 film, the title character, who has become the host of a children's television show, answers this letter from a viewer:

Two months ago my mom and dad decided to separate. Now they live in different houses. My brother says that we aren't a real family any more. Is this true? Did I lose my family? Is there anything I could do to get my parents back together?

Oh, my dear. You know, some parents get along much better when they don't live together. They don't fight all the time and they can become better people. Much better mommies and daddies for you. And sometimes they get back together. And sometimes they don't, dear. And if they don't, don't blame yourself. Just because they don't love each other doesn't mean that they don't love you.

There are all sorts of different families. Some families have one mommy, some families have one daddy, or two families. . . They may not see each other for days, weeks, months or even years at a time. But if there's love, dear, those are the ties that bind. And you'll have a family in your heart forever. All my love to you, poppet. You're going to be all right.[1]

The child's situation is entirely too common in our nation – both within the church and outside of it. But the TV host's answer is striking. The heartwarming music accompanying the words only make them seem more *loving*, more *reasonable*, more *tolerant*. There's just one problem – the TV host never once tells the child the truth – that what has happened to her family is not what God intended for her or for the rest of her family!

Allow me to state what, for the Christian, is the obvious: God is the Author of the family, and His design is not as flexible as the filmmakers would like us to believe. In fact, it's not flexible *at all*. The ideal design for the family has always been a man, his wife and their children. The fact that other family structures exist today doesn't change that fact.

The ideal family structure is what it is because that's how God decided it should be. He didn't ask for your input or mine, because He didn't need our help.

In my work advocating the family and biblical marriage through the Center for Moral Clarity, I'm often asked why I am so adamant that marriage must forever remain the union of one man and one woman under the law. I'm grateful that I don't have to rely on my own understanding for an answer. I can simply point to the Word of God and show where the family originated – in the book of Genesis. Those who argue for the travesties that are polygamy or homosexual marriage, therefore, are not arguing with me, but with God!

Since marriage was instituted by God, He has laws concerning it – laws every believer is required to follow. Marriage is an illustration of man's relationship to God. Fidelity, or faithfulness, is vital in both relationships. God ordained the first marriage a matter of days after creation began:

And God said, Let us make man in our image, after our likeness: and let them have dominion over the fish of the sea, and over the fowl of the air, and over the cattle, and over all the earth, and over every creeping thing that creepeth upon the earth. So God created man in his own image, in the image of God created he him; male and female created he them. And God blessed them, and God said unto them, Be fruitful, and multiply, and replenish the earth, and subdue it: and have dominion over the fish of the sea, and over the fowl of the air, and over every living thing that moveth upon the earth.

—Genesis 1:26-28

Viewing the works of His hands, God created woman in answer to man's needs and ordained the first marriage:

And the Lord God said, It is not good that the man should be alone; I will make him an help meet for him. And out of the ground the Lord God formed every beast of the field, and every fowl of the air; and brought them unto Adam to see what he would call them: and whatsoever Adam called every living creature, that was the name thereof. And Adam gave names to all cattle, and to the fowl of the air, and to every beast of the field; but for Adam there was not found an help meet for him. And the Lord God caused a deep sleep to fall upon Adam and he slept: and he took one of his ribs, and closed up the flesh instead thereof; And the rib, which the Lord God had taken from man, made he a woman, and brought her unto the man. And Adam said, This is now bone of my bones, and flesh of my flesh: she shall be called Woman, because she was taken out of Man. Therefore

shall a man leave his father and his mother, and shall cleave unto his wife: and they shall be one flesh.
                                                            –Genesis 2:18-24

Leaving father and mother – forming a new family unit, rather than an extension of an existing one – is more important for a man than for a woman. The reason is that a man needs to develop independence and strength, so he can be the high priest of his home, as God demands. Solomon affirmed that God approves of marriage between a man and a woman in Proverbs 18:22, *"Whoso findeth a wife findeth a good thing, and obtaineth favour of the Lord."* Jesus also endorsed His Father's model of marriage and family:

But from the beginning of the creation God made them male and female. For this cause shall a man leave his father and mother, and cleave to his wife; And they twain shall be one flesh: so then they are no more twain, but one flesh. What therefore God hath joined together, let not man put asunder.
                                                            –Mark 10:6-9

The Bible also makes clear that marriage between a man and a woman is the only legitimate format for sexual expression. James, brilliantly resolving a dispute about what requirements Gentile converts to Christianity must meet, resolved,

Wherefore my sentence is, that we trouble not them, which from among the Gentiles are turned to God: But that we write unto them, that they abstain from pollutions of idols, ***and from fornication,*** *and from things strangled, and from blood. For Moses*

of old time hath in every city them that preach him, being read in the synagogues every sabbath day.
— *Acts 15:19-21*
(emphasis added)

Fornication, in this context, is *any* sexual activity outside the marriage relationship. This applies equally to sex between a man and a woman and between two members of the same sex; if it's outside the God-ordained family unit of one man and one woman, it is prohibited.

Paul, who never married, likewise acknowledged that sex is reserved for marriage between a husband and wife. He wrote,

Nevertheless, to avoid fornication, let every man have his own wife, and let every woman have her own husband. Let the husband render unto the wife due benevolence: and likewise also the wife unto the husband. The wife hath not power of her own body, but the husband: and likewise also the husband hath not power of his own body, but the wife. Defraud ye not one the other, except it be with consent for a time, that ye may give yourselves to fasting and prayer; and come together again, that Satan tempt you not for your incontinency.
— *1 Corinthians 7:2-5*

Make no mistake, God *encourages* marriage. It is not something He reluctantly provides to satisfy our sexual desires; it is something He intends for our pleasure. God delights in the happiness of His children, and He intends the marriage relationship to be one in which we find happiness.

If you are a parent, what do you want for your children? I'm sure that next to your desire that they be saved, your heart's desire for your children is that they be fulfilled and happy in marriages of their own. God has shown in Scripture that He feels the same about His children: *"Let thy fountain be blessed: and rejoice with the wife of thy youth . . . be thou ravished always with her love."*

−Proverbs 5:18,19b

Other Rules of Marriage

We get a clear idea of how seriously God takes marriage by the use of one word: *covenant*. In the Hebrew, the word we read in the Bible as "covenant" roughly means "to cut where blood flows." The Greek word we translate "covenant" means "contract," a binding legal agreement.

Marriage is a blood covenant. The physical act of consummating a marriage often involves the shedding of blood. With or without this physical symbol, it's clear throughout Scripture that God views marriage as a covenant between a man and a woman:

Yet ye say, Wherefore? Because the Lord hath been witness between thee and the wife of thy youth, against whom thou hast dealt treacherously: yet is she thy companion, and the wife of thy covenant. And did not he make one? Yet had he the residue of the spirit. And wherefore one? That he might seek a godly seed. Therefore take heed to your spirit, and let none deal treacherously against the wife of his youth.

−Malachi 2:14,15

And he answered and said unto them, Have ye not read, that he which made them at the beginning made them male and female, And said, For this cause shall a man leave father and mother, and shall cleave to his wife: and they twain shall be one flesh?

–Matthew 19:4,5

And the Pharisees came to him, and asked him, Is it lawful for a man to put away his wife? tempting him. And he answered and said unto them, What did Moses command you? And they said, Moses suffered to write a bill of divorcement, and to put her away. And Jesus answered and said unto them, For the hardness of your heart he wrote you this precept. But from the beginning of the creation God made them male and female. For this cause shall a man leave his father and mother, and cleave to his wife; And they twain shall be one flesh: so then they are no more twain, but one flesh.

–Mark 10:2-8

God's Word also is clear that marriage is for our time here on earth, not for eternity. Jesus was once approached by a group of Sadducees and challenged with a convoluted question about marriage. They had hoped to trap Jesus into saying something blasphemous, because they did not believe in the resurrection of the dead. But Jesus turned the tables on them by teaching them something they didn't expect:

The same day came to him the Sadducees, which say that there is no resurrection, and asked him, Saying, Master, Moses said, If a man die, having no children, his brother shall marry his wife, and raise up seed unto his brother. Now there were with us seven brethren: and the first, when he had married a wife, deceased, and, having no issue, left his wife unto his brother: Likewise the second also, and the third, unto the seventh. And last of all the woman died also.

Therefore in the resurrection whose wife shall she be of the seven? for they all had her. Jesus answered and said unto them, Ye do err, not knowing the scriptures, nor the power of God. For in the resurrection they neither marry, nor are given in marriage, but are as the angels of God in heaven. But as touching the resurrection of the dead, have ye not read that which was spoken unto you by God, saying, I am the God of Abraham, and the God of Isaac, and the God of Jacob? God is not the God of the dead, but of the living.
—Matthew 22:23-32

God also recognizes that the family is a training ground for leadership. Paul implied as much when he established requirements for liturgical offices in the church:

This is a true saying, If a man desire the office of a bishop, he desireth a good work. A bishop then must be blameless, **the husband of one wife,** *vigilant, sober, of good behaviour, given to hospitality, apt to teach . . . One that ruleth well his own house,* **having his children in subjection with all gravity; (For if a** *man know not how to rule his own house, how shall he take care of the church of God?)*
—1 Timothy 3:1,2,4,5
(emphasis added)

Let the deacons be **the husbands of one wife, ruling their children and their own houses well.** *For they that have used the office of a deacon well purchase to themselves a good degree, and great boldness in the faith which is in Christ Jesus.*
—1 Timothy 3:12,13
(emphasis added)

I'm aware that some evangelical leaders interpret relevant parts of these passages to mean that only men who have never been divorced may serve in the church offices of bishop and deacon. I don't agree with that assessment. Rather, I believe Paul is saying here that a bishop and deacon should be a "one-woman man."

God also places a specific prohibition on who may marry. Specifically, He forbids incest – marriage and sexual relationships between close relatives, and between parent and child.

Incest has many disastrous consequences and, of course, is morally wrong. There are reasons why it is harmful to mankind. The royal families of Europe intermarried for centuries; the result was mental and physical retardation.

God could not be clearer about how He feels about incest in this passage from the book of Leviticus:

> *None of you shall approach to any that is near of kin to him, to uncover their nakedness: I am the Lord. The nakedness of thy father, or the nakedness of thy mother, shalt thou not uncover: she is thy mother; thou shalt not uncover her nakedness. The nakedness of thy father's wife shalt thou not uncover: it is thy father's nakedness. The nakedness of thy sister, the daughter of thy father, or daughter of thy mother, whether she be born at home, or born abroad, even their nakedness thou shalt not uncover. The nakedness of thy son's daughter, or of thy daughter's daughter, even their nakedness thou shalt not uncover: for theirs is thine own nakedness. The nakedness of thy father's wife's daughter, begotten of thy father, she is thy sister, thou shalt not uncover her nakedness. Thou shalt not uncover the nakedness of thy father's sister: she is thy father's near kinswoman. Thou shalt not uncover the nakedness of thy mother's sister: for she is thy mother's*

near kinswoman. Thou shalt not uncover the nakedness of thy father's brother, thou shalt not approach to his wife: she is thine aunt. Thou shalt not uncover the nakedness of thy daughter in law: she is thy son's wife; thou shalt not uncover her nakedness. Thou shalt not uncover the nakedness of thy brother's wife: it is thy brother's nakedness. Thou shalt not uncover the nakedness of a woman and her daughter, neither shalt thou take her son's daughter, or her daughter's daughter, to uncover her nakedness; for they are her near kinswomen: it is wickedness. Neither shalt thou take a wife to her sister, to vex her, to uncover her nakedness, beside the other in her life time.

—Leviticus 18:6-18

There is a spiritual application to this also. Christians need to listen with spiritual ears to the ideas and concepts of people from other backgrounds and groups. If they only hear what is being said by people just like them, they are guilty of spiritual and intellectual incest. That doesn't mean to become gullible, however, and blindly accept anything that comes around. We must be constantly in tune with the Word of God, so we can discern what teaching is and is not biblically based.

Christians must also see with spiritual eyes the new things that God is doing. They must not permit themselves to be bound by the cords of religious tradition, lest they suffer spiritual retardation. This happens when they never assimilate anything but what their particular denomination or group believes.

The Importance of Virginity

Genesis 2:24 states that a man founding a family should "leave and cleave." Men are told to leave their fathers and mothers and cleave unto their wives. The word "cleave" literally means to be joined together in a fashion that would require a surgical procedure to separate. This cleaving takes place at the level of souls, which is why husbands and wives so often refer to their spouse as their "soul mate."

All sexual intimacy involves cleaving – becoming joined not only physically, but also emotionally and mentally. That's why it's so important that sexual activity take place only within the context of a marriage relationship. No matter how casual or brief the relationship, cleaving takes place. When the relationship is not a permanent one, cleaving will either cause profound heartache or numb you until you can't feel anything at all.

When a short-term sexual relationship ends, the resulting separation causes a rip in the fabric of the soul – the mind, will and emotions. That tearing, if not properly dealt with, causes scarring. Scar tissue or adhesions do not have the sensitivity or flexibility of normal tissue, so the result of multiple intimacies is to make it difficult, if not impossible, to cleave to someone else.

Many times I have ministered to men and women who have had multiple sexual partners before finding their future spouse. Their casual sexual experiences, which seemed so unimportant at the time, became like video files permanently embedded in their conscience as they began their marriage. These video files play in their minds whenever they think about their husband or wife, no matter how much they try not to think about their sexual past. Some people can minimize the effect of these images that interfere with their enjoyment of their spouse. Many can't, even though their heart is to think only about their husband or wife as the sole object of their physical desire.

This can be changed by the healing power of God, but it requires openness to God's healing and cleansing power. God understood this. He taught us in His Word that the best thing for us is marriage – one man, one woman, for life.

Please don't misunderstand me. I don't mean to heap condemnation on those who have squandered their virginity before marriage, either in a state of carnality or before they were born again and baptized by the Holy Ghost. God can and will restore you. I've seen it happen more times than I can count. Forgiveness for your past sexual sin is as close as your next prayer. God's best for you, however, is for both partners in a marriage to be virgins on their wedding night. Throughout Scripture, God places a premium on virginity. That's because if there is no value placed on something, it is more likely that its loss will be viewed with apathy. God's instruction list, the book of Deuteronomy, includes these directions:

And, lo, he hath given occasions of speech against her, saying, I found not thy daughter a maid; and yet these are the tokens of my daughter's virginity. And they shall spread the cloth before the elders of the city. And the elders of that city shall take that man and chastise him; And they shall amerce him in an hundred shekels of silver, and give them unto the father of the damsel, because he hath brought up an evil name upon a virgin of Israel: and she shall be his wife; he may not put her away all his days. But if this thing be true, and the tokens of virginity be not found for the damsel: Then they shall bring out the damsel to the door of her father's house, and the men of her city shall stone her with stones that she die: because she hath wrought folly in Israel, to play the whore in her father's house: so shalt thou put evil away from among you.

If a man be found lying with a woman married to an husband, then they shall both of them die, both the man that lay with the woman, and the woman: so shalt thou put away evil from Israel. If a damsel that is a virgin be betrothed unto an husband, and a man find her in the city, and lie with her; Then ye shall bring them both out unto the gate of that city, and ye shall stone them with stones that they die; the damsel, because she cried not, being in the city; and the man, because he hath humbled his neighbour's wife: so thou shalt put away evil from among you.

–Deuteronomy 22:17-24

God showed what a premium He placed on virginity when, in response to prophecy, He chose Mary, a virgin Jewish girl, to be the mother of Jesus. The prophecy is found in Isaiah: *"Therefore the Lord himself shall give you a sign; Behold, a virgin shall conceive, and bear a son, and shall call his name Immanuel" (Isaiah 7:14).*

At the appointed time, Joseph was told of his fiancée's divine destiny this way:

Then Joseph her husband, being a just man, and not willing to make her a publick example, was minded to put her away privily. But while he thought on these things, behold, the angel of the Lord appeared unto him in a dream, saying, Joseph, thou son of David, fear not to take unto thee Mary thy wife: for that which is conceived in her is of the Holy Ghost. And she shall bring forth a son, and thou shalt call his name Jesus: for he shall save his people from their sins. Now all this was done, that it might be fulfilled which was spoken of the Lord by the prophet, saying, Behold, a virgin shall be with child, and shall bring forth a son, and they shall call his name Emmanuel, which being interpreted is, God with us. Then Joseph being raised

*from sleep did as the angel of the Lord had bidden
him, and took unto him his wife: And knew her not till
she had brought forth her firstborn son: and he called
his name Jesus.*

—Matthew 1:19-25

The apostle Paul, in his admonishments on marriage, also emphasizes the importance of virginity. He is careful to separate his opinion from commandment:

*Now concerning the things whereof ye wrote unto me:
It is good for a man not to touch a woman.
Nevertheless, to avoid fornication, let every man have
his own wife, and let every woman have her own
husband. Let the husband render unto the wife due
benevolence: and likewise also the wife unto the
husband. The wife hath not power of her own body,
but the husband: and likewise also the husband hath
not power of his own body, but the wife. Defraud ye
not one the other, except it be with consent for a time,
that ye may give yourselves to fasting and prayer; and
come together again, that Satan tempt you not for
your incontinency. But I speak this by permission, and
not of commandment. For I would that all men were
even as I myself. But every man hath his proper gift of
God, one after this manner, and another after that.*

—1 Corinthians 7:1-7

Some Bible scholars pervert Paul's advice in this passage to mean that God frowns on marriage. Nothing could be further from the truth. While not all Christians should be married, and a sovereign God will require others to wait for marriage far longer than they would prefer, Paul clearly understood that marriage, not singleness, was the natural state for most believers. In Paul's day, the Jewish Christians in and around Jerusalem were facing persecution of an unprecedented scope. A spouse and family, under those circumstances, would be a liability. After the destruction of Jerusalem in 70 A.D., this advice was not as valid as it was at the time it was written.

God's laws regarding marriage are no more flexible than His laws on any other subject. They are not subject to negotiation or a grading scale. They are the expectation of every believer. The fact that God gave us so many rules about marriage means that He places a very high priority on how we form families, and how we behave within them.

The good news is, He created marriage and families for our pleasure. When we treat our spouses and our children with value, as Scripture commands us, they will bring us unspeakable joy, and will give us glimpses of God as He works in our lives.

Chapter Two
The Roles of Husband and Wife

Wives, submit yourselves unto your own husbands, as unto the Lord. For the husband is the head of the wife, even as Christ is the head of the church...Husbands, love your wives, even as Christ also loved the church, and gave himself for it...So ought men to love their wives as their own bodies...For this cause shall a man leave his father and mother, and shall be joined unto his wife, and they two shall be one flesh...Nevertheless let every one of you in particular so love his wife even as himself; and the wife see that she reverence her husband.

—Ephesians 5:22,23,25,28,31,33

Chapter Two
The Roles of Husband and Wife

Few subjects within the church carry more emotional baggage than the roles of husbands and wives in a marriage. In 30 years of ministry I have known husbands who have misread the clear commands of Scripture, creating a tyrannical environment in their homes and justifying it by quoting a single verse from Ephesians 5.

I've also known wives who have rejected outright the notion that they should be submissive to their husbands, because they (correctly) believed that they were their husband's equal.

Both situations are a recipe for disaster, because they represent a misunderstanding of Scripture. A thorough understanding of the whole counsel of God where marriage is concerned is required for a happy, stable family life.

Any team effort can only be effective when everyone on the team understands and fully accepts their assigned roles. In basketball, for example, the player that handles the ball most often is called the point guard; often this player is one of the shorter members of the team. It's the point guard's responsibility to bring the ball up the floor, call the play and make the passes that allow the play to work. When this player gets to shoot, it's often far away from the basket. The center, typically the tallest player on the team, handles the ball occasionally, but more often than not this player's role is to stay close to the basket. That way, if a shot is missed, the player's height makes them better able to rebound the ball.

Nothing is more frustrating for me to see, as a basketball fan, than when the players forsake their assigned roles. The coach doesn't want the center routinely shooting from the outside, because that leaves them in a poor position to rebound. Nor does the coach want the point guard shooting down the floor every time, because their role is to involve everyone else in the play. All five players on the floor are essential to the team's success, but the team functions well only when each player fulfills their assigned role.

God has clearly assigned roles for both members of a Christian marriage. The man is the head of the family, and the wife fulfills a supporting role. Understand that this is an organizational arrangement, and not a judgment of qualifications. Most women I know would claim (and more men than you might guess would readily admit) that their role in the family is not necessarily a reflection of their true abilities compared to those of their spouse!

Gender-role assignments don't make the husband superior to the wife, or vice versa. These roles are simply the way God has decided the family should function. Since He is the creator and we are the creation, our only legitimate response is to follow His commands in this area.

Duties of Husbands

The Bible is full of commands to husbands, all of which are dominated by admonitions to love their wives. It's been that way since the Garden of Eden:

And Adam said, This is now bone of my bones, and flesh of my flesh: she shall be called Woman, because she was taken out of Man. Therefore shall a man leave his father and his mother, and shall cleave unto his wife: and they shall be one flesh.

–Genesis 2:23,24

Solomon also emphasized a man's requirement to be pure before God, and to be exclusively satisfied with the love of his wife:

Drink waters out of thine own cistern, and running waters out of thine own well. Let thy fountains be dispersed abroad, and rivers of waters in the streets. Let them be only thine own, and not strangers' with thee. Let thy fountain be blessed: and rejoice with the wife of thy youth. Let her be as the loving hind and pleasant roe; let her breasts satisfy thee at all times; and be thou ravished always with her love.

—*Proverbs 5:15-19*

Live joyfully with the wife whom thou lovest all the days of the life of thy vanity, which he hath given thee under the sun, all the days of thy vanity: for that is thy portion in this life, and in thy labour which thou takest under the sun.

—*Ecclesiastes 9:9*

Elsewhere in the New Testament, we see that God takes very seriously the requirement of men to be faithful to the marriage covenant. God is the overseer of your marriage, men, and He will not excuse your failure to observe your covenant! Hear these words:

Yet ye say, Wherefore? Because **the Lord hath been witness between thee and the wife of thy youth,** *against whom thou hast dealt treacherously: yet is she thy companion, and the wife of thy covenant. And did not he make one? Yet had he the residue of the spirit. And wherefore one? That he might seek a godly seed. Therefore take heed to your spirit, and let none deal treacherously against the wife of his youth. For the Lord, the God of Israel, saith that he hateth putting away: for one covereth violence with his garment,* *saith the Lord of hosts: therefore take heed to your spirit, that ye deal not treacherously.*

–Malachi 2:14-16
(emphasis added)

The most comprehensive passage of Scripture in the Bible relating to marriage roles is found in Ephesians 5. Here's what Paul says about the husband's role:

*Wives, submit yourselves unto your own husbands, as unto the Lord. **For the husband is the head of the wife,** even as Christ is the head of the church: and he is the saviour of the body. Therefore as the church is subject unto Christ, so let the wives be to their own husbands in every thing. **Husbands, love your wives, even as Christ also loved the church, and gave himself for it;** That he might sanctify and cleanse it with the washing of water by the word, That he might present it to himself a glorious church, not having spot, or wrinkle, or any such thing; but that it should be holy and without blemish. **So ought men to love their wives as their own bodies.** He that loveth his wife loveth himself. For no man ever yet hated his own flesh; but nourisheth and cherisheth it, even as the Lord the church: For we are members of his body, of his flesh, and of his bones. For this cause shall a man leave his father and mother, and shall be joined unto his wife, and **they two shall be one flesh.** This is a great mystery: but I speak concerning Christ and the church. Nevertheless let every one of you in particular so love his wife even as himself; and the wife see that she reverence her husband.*

–Ephesians 5:22-33
(emphasis added)

At least three points are worth noting here. First, husbands are to love their wives just as much as Christ loved the church. Jesus died for the Church on Calvary's rugged cross; husbands are to be willing to do nothing less for their wives.

Second, men are clearly admonished to love their wives as their own bodies – because in God's eyes, that's exactly what they are. Paul paraphrases Genesis 2:24 to emphasize this point.

Third, the husband is the "head" of the wife, but do we really know what that means? In the 21st century business world, we think of the "head" of a company or a department as someone with superior rank, who has unquestioned authority to do whatever they see fit regarding those under their command. The biblical text, however, doesn't support such an interpretation of "head" for the husband. Rather, it supports a leader who:

- Takes responsibility for the success of the family.

- Acts without regard for his needs, but with a passion for the needs of his family.

- Maintains a keen awareness of his responsibility for the woman he married and the children God gave them.

- Avoids any behavior that would position himself as a domineering presence in the lives of his wife and children.

It's absolutely critical in Christian families that husbands understand the true nature of their God-given role as the leader of their families. The husband is *not* to be the family's tyrant. In many ways, he is to be its *servant!*

This passage also reminds us clearly of what love is, and

what it isn't. Love is what God *commands* of husbands where their wives are concerned. It is not a feeling that waxes and wanes from day to day, month to month, year to year. Authentic love is not subject to changes in one's attractiveness, physical capabilities, financial prosperity or the children's behavior. It's not even dependent on whether the husband and wife have recently had an argument (or what Christians sometimes euphemistically refer to as "intense fellowship").

God's command in this passage of Scripture has no qualifiers whatsoever. It simply says, "Husbands, love your wives!" Popular secular songwriters have it exactly backward; love is not a feeling. It is an act of will, one that God commands husbands to exercise on behalf of their wives.

Paul elaborates by saying that husbands should love their wives as their own bodies. Very few of us in this image-conscious time truly feel love for our own bodies – but we certainly do take care of them, don't we? We exercise, we watch what we eat, we bathe ourselves, we rest when we're tired, we go to the doctor when we have aches and pains, we take medication to cure our afflictions and most of us even have a favorite chair we sit in after supper! We also attend to these activities continually – they aren't something we do once and then neglect.

If a husband pays as much attention to his wife as he does to the needs of his own body, he will never be frustrated by her response to his leadership of the home. The wife is not placed in the home to give a husband practice in management training; she is given for a husband to love and enjoy. A wife is not an employee – she is a gift from God, and a husband needs to treat her as a gift. As a husband cares for his own body on a continual basis, he needs to be constantly about the business of showing his wife that he loves her as Christ loved the Church.

Duties of Wives

Not long ago, I heard a story that one of the greeting card companies supplied Mother's Day cards to a local correctional institution, so inmates could send cards to their mothers. The available cards were quickly snatched up and mailed. The greeting card company responded the next month by making Father's Day cards available in the same prison, but those cards went nearly untouched.

This story demonstrates the great crisis in our culture with father abandoning their families and abdicating their family responsibilities, but it also speaks to the great importance and influence women have in their homes. Far from a second-class job, the role of the wife is absolutely vital to raising children who know God, love Him, honor Him and serve Him.

Throughout Scripture, God gives detailed instructions about a wife's duties. The first indication that God intended a distinct role for the wife occurred before He created Eve: "*And the Lord God said, It is not good that the man should be alone; I will make him an help meet for him*" *(Genesis 2:18).*

The role of "help meet," rendered "helper" in many biblical translations, itself is controversial. But that's because we're looking at the word through the eyes of modern-day culture. God doesn't intend for a helper to be an insignificant role, because that is a role He assigns to Himself:

> *I will lift up mine eyes unto the hills, from whence cometh my help.* **My help cometh from the Lord,** *which made heaven and earth.*
>
> —*Psalm 121:1,2*
> *(emphasis added)*

Do you think God would call Himself a helper if that were a demeaning job description? I don't think so! If that title is good enough for the Maker of heaven and earth, it should be good enough for anyone.

Perhaps the best-known passage in the Bible on this subject, Proverbs 31, shows that as the keeper of the home, wives have a myriad of duties:

Who can find a virtuous woman? for her price is far above rubies. The heart of her husband doth safely trust in her, so that he shall have no need of spoil. She will do him good and not evil all the days of her life. She seeketh wool, and flax, and worketh willingly with her hands. She is like the merchants' ships; she bringeth her food from afar. She riseth also while it is yet night, and giveth meat to her household, and a portion to her maidens. She considereth a field, and buyeth it: with the fruit of her hands she planteth a vineyard. She girdeth her loins with strength, and strengtheneth her arms. She perceiveth that her merchandise is good: her candle goeth not out by night. She layeth her hands to the spindle, and her hands hold the distaff. She stretcheth out her hand to the poor; yea, she reacheth forth her hands to the needy. She is not afraid of the snow for her household: for all her household are clothed with scarlet. She maketh herself coverings of tapestry; her clothing is silk and purple. Her husband is known in the gates, when he sitteth among the elders of the land. She maketh fine linen, and selleth it; and delivereth girdles unto the merchant. Strength and honour are her clothing; and she shall rejoice in time to come. She openeth her mouth with wisdom; and in her tongue is the law of kindness. She looketh well to the ways of her household, and eateth not the bread of idleness. Her children arise up, and call her blessed; her husband

also, and he praiseth her. Many daughters have done virtuously, but thou excellest them all. Favour is deceitful, and beauty is vain: but a woman that feareth the Lord, she shall be praised. Give her of the fruit of her hands; and let her own works praise her in the gates.
                                                        –Proverbs 31:10-31

Reading this description of the ideal woman is enough to make most people tired. There's certainly nothing boring about this woman's schedule! Her days – and they are long days – begin before the sunrise *("She riseth also while it is yet night")* and end long after it sets *("her candle goeth not out by night")*. She is involved in business and makes sure that her household, including the hired help, is provided for, both in terms of their everyday needs and in special circumstances *("She is not afraid of the snow for her household: for all her household are clothed with scarlet")*. Clearly, this model wife is not one who has time for soap operas and bon-bons!

Proverbs 31 describes a woman whose heart is focused on her home. I don't believe this passage mandates that godly women be stay-at-home wives and mothers, but it does show that above any employment obligations, a wife's priority must be the administration of the household and the support of her husband.

By support, the text is not talking about providing substantive assistance to the husband's employment – although it may be an ideal situation to have the husband and wife work together in a family enterprise. It refers instead to emotional support *("The heart of her husband doth safely trust in her")*. A wife should take an interest in what her husband does for a living. Encourage him; remember that he derives a great part of his identity from his profession, and treat it as a valid use of his time. He probably needs encouragement as much as you do, and he will be much better prepared to deal with challenges elsewhere if he knows he has your support at home.

Paul talks about the roles of wives in two passages that are particularly challenging for women in the modern-day church. His oft-overlooked letter to Titus includes this admonition:

> *But speak thou the things which become sound doctrine: That the aged men be sober, grave, temperate, sound in faith, in charity, in patience. The aged women likewise, that they be in behaviour as becometh holiness, not false accusers, not given to much wine, teachers of good things; That they may teach the young women to be sober,* **to love their husbands, to love their children,** *To be discreet, chaste, keepers at home, good, obedient to their own husbands,* **that the word of God be not blasphemed.**
>
> *–Titus 2:1-5*
> *(emphasis added)*

Notice first of all that Paul considers the roles of men and women to be "sound doctrine." That elevates this text above a mere dispensation of good advice. They are sound biblical principles that Paul equates, at least tacitly, with justification by faith! They are also not subject to shifting with the prevailing winds of public opinion or supposed enlightenment by pop psychologists. They are part of the time-tested, immutable Word of God which, like Jesus Christ, is the same yesterday, today and forever.

This passage in Titus also demonstrates the esteem and respect with which we should treat our elders in the faith, but here I want to especially make note of what Paul wants the elder women to teach the younger – to love their husbands and to love their children. Once again, this love is not to be conditional or dependent on feelings. It is to be present at all times, in all situations, in the midst of all manner of difficulties a family may endure. It is meant to endure even when the doctor gives a bad report, when the factory is downsizing and when there is month left at the end of the money.

If you ever question the importance of your supportive role as a wife and mother, Paul shatters that notion at the end of the passage (*"that the word of God be not blasphemed"*). That's right: a wife's fidelity to her assigned role in the home has eternal consequences! Paul is asserting here that nothing less than the reputation of the Christian faith is at stake when it comes to a wife's behavior in the home. If she publicly demonstrates disdain for her husband, or begrudges the fact that she has children, she is not just slandering members of her family – she is blaspheming the faith she claims as her own!

The biblical model of marriage and family is, unfortunately, increasingly mocked in our society. Paul is emphasizing here that a wife's disobedience to God's Word in this area brings Christianity into disrepute among her extended family, friends and co-workers – the very people her God has given her as a mission field.

The Dreaded "S" Word

Probably no other word draws as much ire when discussing the biblical roles of men and women as does "submission." Feminist dogma, which has invaded many of our churches, has convinced many women that this word means "slavery." It doesn't. A proper understanding of what submission is, and what it means in the context of marriage, is essential to a harmonious Christian marriage.

We've already seen Paul talk about submission in Ephesians 5:

Wives, submit yourselves unto your own husbands, as

*unto the Lord. For the husband is the head of the wife,
even as Christ is the head of the church: and he is the
saviour of the body. Therefore as the church is subject
unto Christ, so let the wives be to their own husbands
in every thing.*

—Ephesians 5:22-24

We've also seen him express much the same thought in the
book of Titus:

*The aged women likewise, that they be in behaviour as
becometh holiness, not false accusers, not given to
much wine, teachers of good things; That they may
teach the young women to be sober, to love their
husbands, to love their children, To be discreet, chaste,
keepers at home, good, obedient to their own
husbands, that the word of God be not blasphemed.*

—Titus 2:3-5

The word "obedient" here is a bad translation; the Greek
word rendered "obedient" in Titus 2 is the same used to arrive
at "submit" in Ephesians 5.

Those who decry the Bible's use of the word
"submission," however, are ignoring an important principle
that Paul introduces before the familiar discussion of familial
roles. It's in Ephesians 5:21: *"Submitting yourselves **one to
another** in the fear of God" (emphasis added)*. In other words,
submission to others is everyone's responsibility! Peter makes
a similar statement in his first epistle:

Likewise, ye younger, submit yourselves unto the elder.

The Roles of Husband and Wife

*Yea, **all of you be subject one to another**, and be clothed with humility: for God resisteth the proud, and giveth grace to the humble.*

–1 Peter 5:5
(emphasis added)

In Ephesians 5, Paul's admonition to wives is simply the first example he gives of a general principle that applies to all believers. He is not relegating women to second-class status; he is simply using a specific example of a universal truth: that believers should esteem one another above themselves. When we are dealing with someone who has authority over us, we are to respond as though Christ Himself were overseeing us.

Get this in your spirit: submission is not a *role*, but a *response*. At one time or another, God requires submission of everyone. In the context of a marriage, God has recognized the leadership role of the man. A wife's submission to her husband is a proper response to her husband's assignment – and it frees him to carry out his responsibility to her and to their children.

Men, don't make a mantra out of Ephesians 5:22 *("Wives, submit yourselves unto your own husbands, as unto the Lord")*. Later in that chapter you are commanded to love your wife just as much as Christ loved the church. Can you think of a greater act of submission than to willingly die for someone else? That's what Christ did for you. A husband has a responsibility to submit to his wife as well, despite his God-ordained position of leadership in the home. A husband should not demand that his wife "get with the program"; instead, he should seek her good at all times. He may be surprised at the favor he'll find in his own home!

Chapter Three
Parents and Children

Couples who plead with God for the privilege of becoming parents...simply want to love another person in the same way they love each other, and to fulfill the longing that God has placed in their hearts to raise up a new generation of blood-bought, sanctified believers in Christ.

Chapter Three
Parents and Children

The Old Testament attitude toward children is accurately reflected in Rachel's words to Jacob in Genesis 30:1: *"Give me children, or I shall die!"*

I have often met with married couples with the same heart's cry Rachel had; their most earnest prayers are for God to allow them to raise a child. As a pastor, there are few moments more enjoyable for me than when a husband and wife who have had difficulty conceiving bring their newborn son or daughter to me for the first time. As a father myself, I know what's ahead for these new families.

By and large these couples who plead with God for the privilege of becoming parents are not breathlessly anticipating teacher conferences, piano recitals, overnight gatherings of friends that are optimistically called "sleepovers," art projects, music lessons, basketball practices, fundraising sales of everything from tubs of frozen cookie dough to Christmas greenery and other routine activities of childhood. They simply want to love another person in the same way they love each other, and to fulfill the longing that God has placed in their hearts to raise up a new generation of blood-bought, sanctified believers in Christ.

Even though some Christian couples are unable to have children together, the Bible is clear that God encourages husbands and wives to have and raise families. As soon as there was a biblical family, God commanded its expansion:

And God blessed them, and God said unto them, Be fruitful, and multiply, and replenish the earth, and subdue it: and have dominion over the fish of the sea, and over the fowl of the air, and over every living thing that moveth upon the earth.

–Genesis 1:28

The book of Psalms also endorses parenthood:

Lo, children are an heritage of the Lord: and the fruit of the womb is his reward. As arrows are in the hand of a mighty man; so are children of the youth. Happy is the man that hath his quiver full of them: they shall not be ashamed, but they shall speak with the enemies in the gate.

–Psalm 127:3-5

It's difficult to overstate the extent to which children were important in Jewish culture. Barrenness – the inability to bear children – was considered a fate worse than death. We've already heard how Rachel cried out for the opportunity to become a mother. Here's the answer to her prayer:

And God remembered Rachel, and God hearkened to her, and opened her womb. And she conceived, and bare a son; and said, God hath taken away my reproach: And she called his name Joseph; and said, The Lord shall add to me another son.

–Genesis 30:22-24

The story of Hannah, the mother of Samuel, is an account of a woman's longing, her prayer of faith, God's faithfulness in answering her prayer, and her faithfulness in performing her vows to God:

Parents and Children

And when the time was that Elkanah offered, he gave to Peninnah his wife, and to all her sons and her daughters, portions: But unto Hannah he gave a worthy portion; for he loved Hannah: but the Lord had shut up her womb. And her adversary also provoked her sore, for to make her fret, because the Lord had shut up her womb. And as he did so year by year, when she went up to the house of the Lord, so she provoked her; therefore she wept, and did not eat....

And Hannah prayed, and said, My heart rejoiceth in the Lord, mine horn is exalted in the Lord: my mouth is enlarged over mine enemies; because I rejoice in thy salvation. There is none holy as the Lord: for there is none beside thee: neither is there any rock like our God. Talk no more so exceeding proudly; let not arrogancy come out of your mouth: for the Lord is a God of knowledge, and by him actions are weighed. The bows of the mighty men are broken, and they that stumbled are girded with strength. They that were full have hired out themselves for bread; and they that were hungry ceased: so that the barren hath born seven; and she that hath many children is waxed feeble.

The Lord killeth, and maketh alive: he bringeth down to the grave, and bringeth up. The Lord maketh poor, and maketh rich: he bringeth low, and lifteth up. He raiseth up the poor out of the dust, and lifteth up the beggar from the dunghill, to set them among princes, and to make them inherit the throne of glory: for the pillars of the earth are the Lord's, and he hath set the world upon them. He will keep the feet of his saints, and the wicked shall be silent in darkness; for by strength shall no man prevail. The adversaries of the Lord shall be broken to pieces; out of heaven shall he thunder upon them: the Lord shall judge the ends of the earth; and he shall give strength unto his king, and exalt the horn of his anointed. And Elkanah went to Ramah to his house. And the child did minister unto the Lord before Eli the priest.

—1 Samuel 1:4-7, 2:1-11

Hannah's song of praise and joy shows the importance placed on children in the Jewish home during Old Testament times. Is it any wonder that when God came to earth, He came first as a baby?

Mary's psalm of praise when she learned she would be the human mother of Jesus certainly was motivated by her knowledge of Who her son would grow to become, but it just as surely was sung out of joy because she was going to be a mother:

And Mary said, My soul doth magnify the Lord, And my spirit hath rejoiced in God my Saviour. For he hath regarded the low estate of his handmaiden: for, behold, from henceforth all generations shall call me blessed. For he that is mighty hath done to me great things; and holy is his name. And his mercy is on them that fear him from generation to generation. He hath shewed strength with his arm; he hath scattered the proud in the imagination of their hearts. He hath put down the mighty from their seats, and exalted them of low degree. He hath filled the hungry with good things; and the rich he hath sent empty away. He hath holpen his servant Israel, in remembrance of his mercy; As he spake to our fathers, to Abraham, and to his seed for ever.

—Luke 1:46-55

During His earthly ministry, Jesus showed a special fondness for children and recommended their qualities of openness and innocence to all of His followers:

And they brought young children to him, that he should touch them: and his disciples rebuked those that brought them. But when Jesus saw it, he was much displeased, and said unto them, Suffer the little children to come unto me, and forbid them not: for of such is the kingdom of God. Verily I say unto you, Whosoever shall not receive the kingdom of God as a little child, he shall not enter therein. And he took them up in his arms, put his hands upon them, and blessed them.

–Mark 10:13-16

And they brought unto him also infants, that he would touch them: but when his disciples saw it, they rebuked them. But Jesus called them unto him, and said, Suffer little children to come unto me, and forbid them not: for of such is the kingdom of God.

–Luke 18:15,16

Instructions for Children

Just as the Bible gives instructions to husbands and wives, it provides admonitions to both parents and children. The most important rule for children is extremely straightforward: *"Honour thy father and thy mother: that thy days may be long upon the land which the Lord thy God giveth thee" (Exodus 20:12).* Notice there is no statute of limitations on this commandment – it is a requirement until the death of the child or of the parents, whichever comes first.

Extreme disobedience of this law was punishable by death during Moses' time: *"And he that smiteth his father, or his mother, shall be surely put to death" (Exodus 21:15).*

FAMILY BEYOND LIMITS

For every one that curseth his father or his mother shall be surely put to death: he hath cursed his father or his mother; his blood shall be upon him.

—Leviticus 20:9

If a man have a stubborn and rebellious son, which will not obey the voice of his father, or the voice of his mother, and that, when they have chastened him, will not hearken unto them: Then shall his father and his mother lay hold on him, and bring him out unto the elders of his city, and unto the gate of his place; And they shall say unto the elders of his city, This our son is stubborn and rebellious, he will not obey our voice; he is a glutton, and a drunkard. And all the men of his city shall stone him with stones, that he die: so shalt thou put evil away from among you; and all Israel shall hear, and fear.

—Deuteronomy 21:18-21

Of course, as any parent will tell you, obedience is a learned behavior for children. If you want your children to disobey you, don't teach them anything, because disobedience will come naturally to them: *"Foolishness is bound in the heart of a child; but the rod of correction shall drive it far from him" (Proverbs 22:15).*

The wicked are estranged from the womb: they go astray as soon as they be born, speaking lies. Their poison is like the poison of a serpent: they are like the deaf adder that stoppeth her ear.

—Psalm 58:3,4

Instructions for Parents

Disobedience is just one more manifestation of the fall. (See Romans 5:12-21.) To instill a spirit of obedience into a child requires diligent training – and if you are a mother or a father, you have been assigned the task of their trainer. It's a non-transferable, unpaid job with unrelenting hours and no possibility of vacation time – and it is the most important role you will ever fulfill on this earth.

Parental discipline is the only way children can be taught to obey. It is your mission, whether you choose to accept it or not.

Scripture is crystal-clear regarding parental responsibilities in this matter. Proverbs mentions it in two different passages: *"He that spareth his rod hateth his son: but he that loveth him chasteneth him betimes" (Proverbs 13:24).*

Withhold not correction from the child: for if thou beatest him with the rod, he shall not die. Thou shalt beat him with the rod, and shalt deliver his soul from hell .
–Proverbs 23:13,14

The text here is calling for firm correction, not flogging a child so that an injury results. Don't you dare look at the word "beat" through your twenty-first century eyes and imagine that the Bible suggests violence against children. Please hear this: the Bible is not advocating child abuse, and neither am I. The "rod" referred to in these Scriptures would be a thin, flexible branch of a tree, what we called a "switch" when I was growing up. It would hurt enough to leave an impression on the mind, but not on the body. It was never intended as an instrument of injury.

A switch was far less likely to wound a child than the hand or any other object.

It's clear from Scripture that much, if not all, of the responsibility for training children in biblical times fell on the mother. The best evidence of this is found in Proverbs 31:1, *"The words of king Lemuel, the prophecy that his mother taught him."*

Paul, in his letters to Timothy, implies that his young son in the faith was instructed by his mother:

> *When I call to remembrance the unfeigned faith that is in thee, which dwelt first in thy grandmother Lois, and thy mother Eunice; and I am persuaded that in thee also.*
> *–2 Timothy 1:5*

> *And that from a child thou hast known the holy scriptures, which are able to make thee wise unto salvation through faith which is in Christ Jesus.*
> *–2 Timothy 3:15*

This is not to say that the father has no role in their children's instruction. To the contrary, because God has assigned the man to be the head of the family, discipline is his ultimate responsibility.

One of the most important instructions for Christian living in all of the New Testament is addressed to fathers, although I believe it applies equally to both parents: *"And, ye fathers, provoke not your children to wrath: but bring them up in the nurture and admonition of the Lord"* (Ephesians 6:4). The Greek word rendered "fathers" in this passage is rendered elsewhere in Scripture as "parents." (See Hebrews 11:23.) Clearly, the instructions here would seem to apply equally to both mothers and fathers.

I can't overstate how important this verse of Scripture is! Faithfully practiced, it will set a child upon a proper course for successful living. It will guide you in raising your daughters to be godly women and your sons to be godly men, with no confusion about their sexual identities. This verse includes two directives:

1. "Provoke not your children to wrath." Paul wrote these words immediately after he wrote about mutual submission, which we studied in the last chapter. This part of the verse, therefore, is a natural extension of that passage. Yes, moms and dads, you are to consider the good of your children in every decision you make!

This verse almost certainly raised some eyebrows in Ephesus when Paul's letter first arrived. In Paul's day, fathers ruled over their families with unquestioned authority. Wives and children were little more than the patriarch's property. So the idea that parents should regard their children as something more than property would have turned the conventional wisdom on its ear. But remember, the context in Paul's admonition to all believers: *"Submitting yourselves one to another in the fear of God" (Ephesians 5:21).*

Here are some practical applications of what Paul meant:

• **Don't be too quick or too harsh with punishment.** If your children are forever tiptoeing around the house, afraid that they will do something that will earn them some form of disciplinary action, they will ultimately rebel against your authority. Draw the line about what you will and will not accept, and enforce that line consistently. For example, some parents choose not to battle with their children about the cleanliness of their room (as long as they can close the door), but are strict about messes in the areas of the house that all family members share, such as the living room. Please note that I am not suggesting that you abdicate your responsibility to provide firm discipline on important matters – I am merely suggesting that you choose your battles wisely.

• **Be consistent.** The same misbehavior should be corrected every time, in a predictable manner, and should be the same for all children in the family. In addition, the disciplinary action taken should fit the crime. Grounding an older child, for example, will feel like as much a punishment of you as it is of your child. Make sure the offense is worth the misery.

- **Don't play favorites!** The story of Jacob and Esau (Genesis 25 and 27) provides a cautionary tale all parents should heed. Isaac preferred Esau over Jacob. His wife, Rebekah, favored Jacob. Their favoritism led to a permanent split in the family. Jacob later favored one of his sons, Joseph, over the others, which led to Joseph's eventual captivity.

- **Don't discourage your children.** Your words can wound your children. I have had many accomplished adults confess to me that they have always felt inferior because one parent or the other called them stupid or told them they would never amount to anything. They literally break down in tears over words their parents said to them decades earlier. Parents, the words you speak to your children today will likely affect them the rest of their lives – why wouldn't you make sure you were speaking words of affirmation, not of condemnation?

2. "Bring them up in the nurture and admonition of the Lord." The biblical model of the family is under unrelenting attack today from groups that would destroy it. Some of these groups make no pretense about their goal to permanently alter the meaning of family and gender roles in this nation. Others may be well meaning, but are surely misguided in their desire to adapt family structures to the times in which we live. Only the discipline and instruction of the Lord – training about the One who is the same yesterday, today and forever – will prepare your children adequately for developing a harmonious family of their own as adults. Proper training also will assure that your daughters learn what it means to be feminine and your sons to be masculine.

Our children can view assaults on the Christian faith every time they turn on the television or log on to the Internet. If they attend public school, they may well be taught by a member of the National Education Association who feels a special calling to teach students about tolerance and understanding of all different forms of sexual perversion.

There's one antidote to all this craziness – you, and your commitment to bring up your children in the nurture and admonition of the Lord. When you take seriously your call to lead your family and diligently train your children in what the Word of God says about husbands and wives, children and parents, they will ultimately understand that your lessons constitute truth – and the truth will free them from a debauched lifestyle that dishonors God.

Your assignment to train up your children in the way they should go requires an intentional, strategic effort. It is time consuming and intellectually demanding – and well worth it. Here are some suggestions for demonstrating the importance of a godly lifestyle to your children:

Date Your Children. From the time your children are old enough to carry on a conversation, both moms and dads should devote one-on-one time with each of them. It could be a Saturday-morning breakfast at McDonald's, a fishing trip or a private appointment in your study. Regardless, each date should be your time alone with your child, and it should be purposeful. Begin this discipline as soon as you can, and start with the essentials of the faith. Then teach them about the life of Jesus, the stories of the early church and so on. When they are old enough to study current events at school, turn your conversations to how your Christian worldview informs your understanding of the headlines in your daily newspaper.

This time together should become such a part of your family life that when the time comes to explain how your son or daughter is to relate to a member of the opposite sex, it won't feel nearly as awkward as if you had never had a serious conversation before.

Mothers and fathers, it is your responsibility to witness your faith to your children, and your "dates" are times when your son or daughter will have your undivided attention. Take advantage of it, and it will pay lifelong dividends.

Demonstrate Your Faith. Never let an opportunity go by to show your children that your relationship with Jesus Christ is the most important thing about you. Pray with them and for them. Let them know that your time of personal prayer and devotions is your private time with God, and that you shouldn't be disturbed. Take them with you to community outreach events and other opportunities to put your faith in action (be sure that smaller children can safely participate or observe first).

If you are called to a specific area of ministry you cannot share with your children (hospital visits or prison ministry, for example), be sure your children know why you are involved in these endeavors. Don't let it be another time that Mom and Dad are away that your children (and your spouse) could grow to resent.

Provide a Christian Education for Your Children. It's no secret that public education has become a factory for liberal ideology, much of which openly ridicules Christianity. I know many devoted teachers and administrators who serve God by working in the public schools, but you shouldn't send your children there unless it's absolutely necessary. There are three excellent options to traditional public education:

- *Bricks-and-mortar Christian schools.* They are available in many communities. I'm proud to have been involved in Christian education for more than 20 years now. We have been able to provide a Christ-centered curriculum for a reasonable tuition rate. If your community has a Christian school, investigate it to make sure it has a spirit of excellence about it. Do not accept an inferior education just because it is "Christian."

• *Charter schools.* Many states have privately operated bricks-and-mortar schools that are serious about instilling traditional values into their students, and they welcome parental participation. They are tuition-free to your family because they receive their funding from the local school district where you live. Because they receive public money, they cannot be distinctively Christian, but it is an important step away from the liberal dogma found in today's public education. It's important to note that nothing prevents you from supplementing their curriculum with Christian training you provide. Another option is online charter schools, which are a de facto home schooling option with tuition paid by the state; many even offer computer hardware and software. Again, be sure to investigate the charter schools available in your area, and do not settle for anything less than academic excellence for your children.

• *Online Christian schools.* This option compares the best elements of bricks-and-mortar Christian schools and online charter schools. Our online school, Harvest Prep Virtual Academy, is available across the nation, at tuition rates far below bricks-and-mortar Christian schools, and features a Christ-centered curriculum and anointed teachers that can help you administer your child's education. More information is available at our Internet site, www.harvestprepva.org.

Any of these three options will require an investment on

your part of time or money or both. In other words, it will require sacrifice. The question I want to ask you is, aren't your children worth that sacrifice? To afford Christian school tuition you may have to vacation in the backyard or keep your vehicles longer than you would like or live in a smaller house than you could otherwise afford. That can be frustrating! Based on the testimonies of parents who have scrimped and saved to afford tuition to our school, I can confidently tell you that the sacrifice is worth it.

Love your spouse. The noted youth pastor Josh McDowell says that the question that gives kids today the most anxiety is not "Does my dad love me?" or "Does my mom love me?" It's "Do my mom and my dad love each other?" Divorce is an epidemic in our society – and as I discussed in the previous chapter, the church is far from immune. Be intentional about your love and respect for your spouse in the presence of your children. You'll be communicating the fact that both of you are committed to each other and to your family, and that will bring your children an unspeakable peace about the stability of their home.

Finally, parents, let me emphasize that it is your responsibility to **share the Gospel with your children.** You must not delegate this duty to children's ministers, Christian school teachers, day-care providers, youth pastors or anyone else! Your children should see you as a sold-out Christian and a work in progress. It's not enough for you to simply model your faith! Your implicit example must be only part of the story you tell to your children about Christianity. You must also provide faith lessons which are explicit, showing them clearly the way to salvation. It's often said that God has children, but no grandchildren. You must not assume that your kids will become believers because you are!

Parents, you have the best opportunity to teach Kingdom living for the next generation of believers, and you have no excuse not to take advantage of it!

Chapter Four
Help for Single-Parent Families

You can not only recover from divorce but, also move closer to God than at any other time in your life.

Chapter Four
Help for Single-Parent Families

On a recent Sunday morning, the Holy Spirit impressed upon me to minister to single mothers. I asked all the women in the congregation who were raising one or more children by themselves to come forward. Instantly our altar area was flooded with women who had endured one of the most emotionally devastating experiences this world has to offer – divorce.

To that group, I prophetically said, "Stop looking for another man! Jehovah Jireh is your provider, your answer, your need-meeter, your companion, your lover!" I encouraged them with the Word of God from the Old and New Testaments:

> *God is not a man, that he should lie; neither the son of man, that he should repent: hath he said, and shall he not do it? or hath he spoken, and shall he not make it good? Behold, I have received commandment to bless: and he hath blessed; and I cannot reverse it. He hath not beheld iniquity in Jacob, neither hath he seen perverseness in Israel: the Lord his God is with him, and the shout of a king is among them.*
> *—Numbers 23:19-21*

> *Remember that Jesus Christ of the seed of David was raised from the dead according to my gospel: Wherein I suffer trouble, as an evil doer, even unto bonds; but the word of God is not bound. Therefore I endure all things for the elect's sakes, that they may also obtain*

the salvation which is in Christ Jesus with eternal glory. It is a faithful saying: For if we be dead with him, we shall also live with him: **If we suffer, we shall also reign with him:** *if we deny him, he also will deny us: If we believe not, yet he abideth faithful: he cannot deny himself.*

–2 Timothy 2:8-13
(emphasis added)

There was rejoicing throughout the tabernacle – the entire congregation celebrating the goodness of our God and His love for these women. I know they returned to their seats more determined than ever not to attach their hopes and dreams for the future to a man who will frequently need to say "I'm sorry" to them. Instead, they left the altar area more determined than ever to embrace the Christ who will never have to apologize for His treatment of them!

That night, the elder who led our service asked for everyone who was raised in a single-parent home to stand. At least a third of the congregation rose – possibly as many as half. The number included many of the most accomplished men and women in our local church. They stood as a profound testimony of the hope that exists for single-parent families.

In each case, I was overwhelmed with the tangible evidence of the devastation that divorce brings to families (let me state here that I realize that many men lead single-parent families as well, but obviously the vast majority of them are headed by women). If that devastation occurs within the church, how much more must it exist in the secular world, among men and women who do not have an eternal connection with a God who will sustain them through the darkest periods of their lives?

Surviving the Epidemic of Divorce

It shouldn't surprise anyone reading this book that divorce is rampant in the secular world. What may surprise you is that within the church of Jesus Christ, the situation is no better! Noted Christian researcher George Barna first shared this stunning finding a decade ago: born-again Christians have the same likelihood of divorce as non-Christians. That fact has been validated in all of the tracking studies Barna's organization has conducted each year since, most recently in 2004[1].

More than a third of married born-again Christians – 35 percent – have experienced a divorce. That's the exact same figure among married adults who are not born again. Among Protestants, the figure is even higher – 39 percent. Among Protestant groups, those most likely to get divorced were white Pentecostals[2]. Clearly, there is a problem in our congregations that the church isn't meeting!

These statistics should give you pause; they certainly disturb me. The good Gospel news I have for those who are living with divorce is that while there is no pain-free way through what you are experiencing, you will get through it because of your relationship with Jesus Christ. He provides the only path that will provide you with true healing.

God will cure you of the anger, frustration and depression you feel, but it will take time and the support of loving Christian friends[3]. Many experts in the field of divorce recovery say it takes an average of one year to recover from a divorce for every five years of marriage before the divorce. The problem church people have with that reality is that they expect God to fix their situation *right now*. But rest assured, He knows what He's doing; He's preparing you for the next phase of your life, which may or may not include a subsequent marriage.

FAMILY BEYOND LIMITS

A woman on our staff who has experienced divorce once told me, "Emotionally, it's like having open-heart surgery. You have to give yourself time to heal and recover. You wouldn't run a marathon immediately after physically having open-heart surgery, so you shouldn't expect to be back to normal – whatever that is – right after getting a divorce."

A person whose life is running more or less normally distributes their energy relatively equally in four different areas – the physical, the mental, the emotional and the spiritual. When you're going through a divorce, though, you are typically expending more than 80 percent of your energy dealing with emotions, instead of 25 percent. One reason single parents are exhausted all the time is because they expend huge amounts of emotional energy just to get through each day, and their physical energy is channeled into caring for their children. If they feel they have nothing left for anything else in their lives, it's because often they don't!

Christian men and women who endure divorce lose something immeasurably more important than a spouse. They also lose the dream of a family life that pleases God and is personally rewarding. If they are part of an active local church, all the programs that focus on children and (intact) families reinforce the feeling that their family situation doesn't please God. In many ways, divorce is the death that keeps on dying, because there are always so many reminders of the way life used to be or the way we think our lives should be. The holiday season is an especially painful time for divorced men and women, because all around are reminders of intact families celebrating together. A single mother may be especially devastated at Christmas, because at a time when she wants her children with her most of all, they will often leave for a visit with their father.

There are other losses in divorce, to be sure. They may include the acceptance of a church family that views a broken home as a black mark on the Body of Christ. In many cases, the loss of friends and family relationships also follow a divorce or dissolution. But it's the death of a dream, whatever form it takes, that can be the most devastating part of enduring a divorce, and the most difficult to regain.

Hear me now: *you can get the dream back* — as well as lots of other things you may have lost. You can not only recover from divorce, but also move closer to God than at any other time in your life.

Make Like Lazarus

How do you recover from a divorce and rebuild a new life for you and your children? I believe we have a model for recovery in the story of Lazarus, found in the 11th chapter of John:

Jesus therefore again groaning in himself cometh to the grave. It was a cave, and a stone lay upon it. Jesus said, Take ye away the stone. Martha, the sister of him that was dead, saith unto him, Lord, by this time he stinketh: for he hath been dead four days. Jesus saith unto her, Said I not unto thee, that, if thou wouldest believe, thou shouldest see the glory of God? Then they took away the stone from the place where the dead was laid. And Jesus lifted up his eyes, and said, Father, I thank thee that thou hast heard me. And I knew that thou hearest me always: but because of the people which stand by I said it, that they may believe that thou hast sent me. And when he thus had spoken, he cried with a loud voice, Lazarus, come forth. And he that was dead came forth, bound hand and foot with graveclothes: and his face was bound about with a napkin. Jesus saith unto them, Loose him, and let him go.

–John 11:38-44

Lazarus is a good model for our study of surviving a divorce or other setback for several reasons:

1. Lazarus was not revived by his own power. Lazarus' resurrection was a miracle of Jesus Christ. It most certainly was not a work of Lazarus.

You cannot in your own strength recover from divorce any more than you can accomplish anything else outside of His grace and other gifts. There is a great freedom in that knowledge, precisely because trying to make it on your own is so confining.

If you are a new Christian, or if you have only been walking with the Lord for a few years, you may be trying to muster your own emotional and spiritual resources to come back to a place where you feel like a vibrant human being again. You may struggle with all your might just to get through each day. I understand those feelings, because I have ministered to people who have endured divorce. The good news is that it doesn't have to be that way.

God still works miracles. He has already worked a miracle in your life, because you have made it through thus far, and He is waiting for you to start what He has finished. No matter how far you've strayed from Him or how depressed you are today, He is attentive to your cry.

2. Lazarus was obedient. Christ performed a miracle in Lazarus' life, but Lazarus chose to emerge from the cave. He was willing to deal with the ramifications of being healed.

You have to be *willing* to be healed from divorce. It is easy to nurse the hurt that comes from a shattered marriage, because it provides a ready-made excuse for any other misfortune you may encounter in the future. People sympathize with you when they know you are going through a divorce. And as difficult as it may be to admit, that sympathy feels good. You may appreciate it precisely because it represents consideration for your feelings that you didn't receive during your marriage.

I am not in any way minimizing the feelings of validation you may receive in the midst of your separation and divorce. They are part of God's healing in your life – but only a part. He will also work directly in your life, so you may someday be able to become the man or woman He created you to be.

There are times when each of us needs to be ministered to by the Body of Christ. Living in the immediate aftermath of a divorce is certainly one of those times. But there is a purpose for that ministering, and it is so we can be effective servants of God again. It's okay to be someone's *ministry* on a temporary basis, as long as you never forget that your ultimate purpose is to be a *minister*.

At some point, God will call on us to progress in our healing so that we can serve others. You may be called to a new marriage, regardless of any fears you may have that you will ultimately be rejected as you were by your former spouse. As you learn that His grace is sufficient for you, you will be able to let go of your fears and be the man or woman of God you are capable of being.

God wants to completely heal His children and make them whole again; He loves us that much. Accepting that love and that healing is not automatic; it takes an act of the will. In cases where healing involves a new marriage, it also requires a significant measure of courage.

3. Lazarus was dependent on others to begin his new life. Jesus commanded Mary, Martha and the mourners gathered around Lazarus' tomb to take off his graveclothes. We know they did so because John later records a dinner in Bethany at which Lazarus sits at the table with Jesus. (See John 12:2.)

God will bring people into your life to help you recover from divorce and enter in to whatever new opportunities He has planned for you.

It's natural to want to withdraw from others when you are separated or divorced. We live in a couples-oriented society, and as a single person you can easily feel like a spare part. But if one of the purposes of the Body of Christ is to minister to its members in need (and it is), then you need to allow the Body to minister to *you* when *you* are in need. To do otherwise is to say that you don't need an essential part of the healing that God has provided for you. Most people I know who have been through a divorce will tell you that they needed all the healing God can provide. It requires great vulnerability to admit to going through a divorce and asking for help, but it is essential.

4. Lazarus was a part of God's plan for revealing Himself to others. Just before this story is the shortest verse in the Bible, *"Jesus wept" (John 11:35)*. He shed tears in the presence of others even though He knew that Lazarus would soon be alive, and that there would almost certainly be rejoicing over that fact. So why did He weep? Perhaps because Lazarus was raised not only for Lazarus' sake, but also for the sake of those in Bethany who witnessed his raising.

Jesus had His own purpose for working this miracle. He had told the disciples that Lazarus was dead and that this would give them another opportunity to believe in Him. (See John 11:15.) We can only speculate about other reasons why Lazarus was raised, but consider this: Jesus' tears were profound evidence of His humanity. Undoubtedly He felt compassion for those who missed Lazarus. And as a result, He did something that doesn't come naturally to most men; He cried. Writing this account some 50 years after Jesus' resurrection and ascension, John found that detail important enough to include in his gospel.

One of the most important messages of this episode from Christ's life is that He hurts when we hurt. That's a great thing to know about God, isn't it? When you are so lonely you could stay in your apartment for months at a time, surviving on frozen food and pizza deliveries, God hurts with you. When you are wounded by your estranged spouse's legal maneuvers, God feels your pain. When your tears stain the divorce papers as you sign them, God weeps with you.

God will teach you many things about Himself, and yourself, in the aftermath of your divorce. But it's important to remember that He will also teach others about Himself through your life. Remember, an important way God teaches us about Himself is through others. In the midst of your trials, do not discount the possibility that He will use your life to teach others about Him.

As you recover from your divorce, know that God is willing to show you a life that is more fulfilling than you could possibly imagine. You can come back to life as Lazarus did, and discover possibilities that never would have been opened to you in any other way.

Other Ways to Heal

Here are some other suggestions for coping with life as a single parent:

1. Be honest with God. The book of Psalms encompasses the panorama of human emotions. That tells me it's okay for you to tell God what you are feeling and how you are hurting. You won't be surprising Him; He already knows your feelings and your thoughts. He is your heavenly Father – the Daddy you can run to and tell anything – and He will always listen to His child, just as He listened to Asaph:

> *I cried unto God with my voice, even unto God with my voice; and he gave ear unto me. In the day of my trouble I sought the Lord: my sore ran in the night, and ceased not: my soul refused to be comforted. I*

*remembered God, and was troubled: I complained,
and my spirit was overwhelmed.*

                                                    –Psalm 77:1-3

Often when you despair you discover how to wait
patiently for the Lord. He always answers! I'm convinced that
being honest with your thoughts and feelings, whether you are
dealing with anger or loneliness or any emotion in between, is
the first step toward receiving the solution God has for you.

2. Reach out to God and His Church. I can't imagine
any man or woman properly healing from a divorce – and it
can be a lifelong process – without Jesus Christ in his or her
life. A non-Christian simply doesn't have the spiritual
resources required to sustain such a trauma. I want to
encourage you to let your needs be known to your pastor or
the leadership of your church. Perhaps there is a divorce
recovery program available at your church or elsewhere in
your community. It will help you a great deal to find
fellowship with those who will best understand your journey,
whether or not they are on the same path you are.

The story of Jesus healing the lame man at Bethesda is so
relevant for single parents:

*After this there was a feast of the Jews; and Jesus went
up to Jerusalem. Now there is at Jerusalem by the
sheep market a pool, which is called in the Hebrew
tongue Bethesda, having five porches. In these lay a
great multitude of impotent folk, of blind, halt,
withered, waiting for the moving of the water. For an
angel went down at a certain season into the pool, and
troubled the water: whosoever then first after the
troubling of the water stepped in was made whole of
whatsoever disease he had. And a certain man was
there, which had an infirmity thirty and eight years.*

*When Jesus saw him lie, and knew that he had been
now a long time in that case, he saith unto him,* **Wilt
thou be made whole?** *The impotent man answered
him, Sir, I have no man, when the water is troubled, to
put me into the pool: but while I am coming, another
steppeth down before me. Jesus saith unto him, Rise,
take up thy bed, and walk. And immediately the man
was made whole, and took up his bed, and walked: and
on the same day was the sabbath.*

–John 5:1-9
(emphasis added)

You have to *want* to recover from the trauma of divorce
and the pain of raising children without a wife or a husband.
You have to decide that you aren't going to wallow in your
grief any more. You have to let God heal you from the pain of
divorce. You have to answer "Yes!" when He asks you, "Do
you want to get well?"

3. Forgive <u>everyone</u> responsible for your divorce.
Now I've started meddling, haven't I? Yet, I don't think you
can fully recover from a divorce unless you have forgiven
everyone involved in the situation – including yourself.

Just after teaching His disciples the model we know as the
Lord's Prayer, Jesus said,

*For if ye forgive men their trespasses, your heavenly
Father will also forgive you: But if ye forgive not men
their trespasses, neither will your Father forgive your
trespasses.*

–Matthew 6:14,15

In other words, forgiving others, including a former
spouse, is required for God to forgive you. I didn't say it was
easy, I just said it was *required*. I know there are probably
ongoing reminders in your life of why you divorced, such as

financial issues or child-custody squabbles. But it is essential to forgive your former spouse for everything that has come between you.

Forgiveness doesn't mean that what your former spouse did to you was acceptable, or that you would even be willing to get back together again if that were a possibility. What it does mean is that you refuse to let your former spouse – and everything he or she did to cause your present situation – dominate your thought life anymore. I once heard that when you refuse to forgive someone, it's like letting him or her live in your head rent-free.

Forgiving that person or persons becomes the only way to evict them from your mind. Make no mistake, forgiveness is absolutely one of the most freeing things you can do.

Notice that I said you need to forgive *everyone* responsible for your divorce. One of the most important people you need to forgive is yourself. If you are a born-again, blood-bought believer, then God has forgiven you for every sin you have ever committed and ever will commit. No matter what you did to contribute to your divorce, in the name of Jesus Christ you are forgiven! That's an incredible reality, but it also means that if you can't forgive yourself, you have higher standards than God!

Get this in your spirit: Christ at Calvary did everything necessary to forgive *all* of your sins, including anything you are responsible for that has led to your present situation. It won't be easy, but God is committed to your healing, and healing can't happen without forgiveness.

Many men and women who are divorced often are ashamed of that fact, because they are a "statistic." Beloved, statistics aren't good or bad, they just *are*. You may not have been in control of whether divorce was part of your story or not, but you *are* in control of how you respond to your situation! Will you use divorce as an excuse, or will you allow God to use your life as a demonstration of His grace, mercy and power?

Chapter Five
Step by Step:
How New Families Can Thrive

In 30 years of ministry, I've seen all kinds of families and stepfamilies. I'm thoroughly convinced that stepfamilies present unique challenges...I'm also convinced that when the husband and the wife are fully submitted to God, and have followed His rules for remarrying in the first place, those stepfamilies can not only survive but thrive!

Chapter Five
Step by Step:
How New Families Can Thrive

A recent book of satire written by a respected Christian humorist has on its cover an illustration of a "typical" Christian family:

- Dad in a golf shirt, with protective arms around Mom and the oldest daughter.
- Mom in a sensible sweater set, with cross necklace and wedding ring prominently positioned.
- Older daughter in a cheerleading outfit, carrying a Teen Study Bible.
- Son in a "Jesus Rocks" T-shirt.
- Younger daughter in a pair of WWJD bib overalls.

A circular cloud, meant to represent a halo, hovers above them. There isn't room for a minivan in the picture, but you just know a family that looks like this owns at least one!

That's the popular picture of the Christian family many people see. It's also the one we often present to the world – a clean, happy, intact, nuclear family, just the way God designed it.

It's rarely that simple, though, isn't it?

Many of the "perfect" families in our churches formed in an entirely different manner. In many families, for example, there is an older daughter, but she was born to Dad and his first wife. She lives with her mother, and visits her father and his new wife on alternate weekends. She loves her dad, but doesn't understand why he left her and her mother five years earlier. She really doesn't understand why Dad didn't make Jesus the focus of his life until two years after that. She often wonders why he couldn't have gotten saved when he and Mom were together.

Big Sis is now more than a little jealous at having to share her father with a younger boy she doesn't really know and an even younger half-sister who demands Dad's attention and that of her stepmother.

The son, meanwhile, lives with his mother and stepfather (the cheerleader's dad). He really likes Mom's new husband, but hesitates to call him Dad because of a sense that he'd be betraying his own father, who now lives in another state and has next to no contact with the boy. So he stubbornly clings to his biological father's surname, which causes his stepfather no small amount of heartache. Dad can't fathom why his stepson would be so loyal to someone who often doesn't want anything to do with him.

The younger daughter, the child of the new union, is somewhat sheltered from the unspoken conflicts that swirl around her. Mom, Dad and her half-siblings realize she doesn't deserve to bear the brunt of the tensions in the family – but that doesn't keep her older brother and sister from resenting the attention she gets from her dad and his mom.

Thanksgiving, Christmas and the Fourth of July are adventures in this family. But those tense times are thankfully few and far between because Mom, Dad and the three children are rarely together all at the same time, since the older daughter lives with her mother and holidays are the few times the son sees his biological father.

Does that sound complicated enough for you? Yet the family unit I've described is one of the simpler configurations of a stepfamily you'll find – what's commonly known as "yours, mine and ours." What if there were more children involved in each spouse's first marriage? What if the current union of man and wife were not the second marriage for both, but the third or fourth, with a child from each relationship? What if the older daughter in the example above now had a stepfather who practiced Islam or Mormonism? Many blended families in our churches today have backstories that are more complicated and include more characters than a *Left Behind* novel.

In 30 years of ministry, I've seen all kinds of families and stepfamilies. I'm thoroughly convinced that stepfamilies present unique challenges, which those of us who are married to our first and only spouse can't begin to fathom. I'm also convinced that when the husband and the wife are fully submitted to God, and have followed His rules for remarrying in the first place, those stepfamilies can not only survive, but thrive!

God's Rules for Divorce and Remarriage

Before a couple in which one or both partners have been previously married, I always ask if the subsequent marriage would be biblical. This isn't a popular practice in the church today, but I will never apologize for modeling my ministry after the teaching of Scripture.

Jesus set the standard for caring about people, but His position on divorce was firm and unambiguous: *"What therefore God hath joined together, let not man put asunder" (Mark 10:9).* It must be so because marriage is unique among all relationships, in that it has been designated by God to serve as a model of His relationship between Jesus and His bride, the Church.

Today's laws allow divorce for the most trivial of reasons, even including "incompatibility." I would submit that on any given day, most of the marriages in this country are incompatible at one time or another! Incompatibility is nothing more than a disagreement that is unresolved. It's nothing less and nothing other than a treatable symptom of temporary discord in a family. Surely it is no reason to permit the destruction of a family, especially when children are involved – children who need the two unique kinds of love that only a mother and a father can provide.

God, in laying the ground rules for marriage, plainly wasn't concerned with trivial, temporal excuses for divorce like "incompatibility." Scripture provides two – and only two – biblical grounds for divorce. One occurs when a believing spouse is abandoned, often by an unbelieving spouse. The apostle Paul wrote, *"But if the unbelieving depart, let him depart. A brother or a sister is not under bondage in such cases: but God hath called us to peace" (1 Corinthians 7:15).*

Beloved, if your spouse walks out on you, with no intention of fulfilling his or her responsibilities to the marriage, the Bible has made divorce an option for you. It's important to note, however, that you <u>are not required</u> to divorce in this situation if you are determined to preserve the marriage. The choice in this situation is yours to make prayerfully, with no threat of condemnation if you reluctantly conclude that divorce is the only course of action remaining for you.

The only grounds for divorce that Jesus mentioned is fornication – habitual sexual relations outside marriage. Jesus said,

> *And I say unto you, Whosoever shall put away his wife, except it be for fornication, and shall marry another, committeth adultery: and whoso marrieth her which is put away doth commit adultery.*
>
> *–Matthew 19:9*

Again, if your spouse has been unfaithful to you, you are *permitted* to seek a divorce, but you are not by any means *required* to do so. In fact, preserving a marriage that has been healed of a spouse's rebellion through fornication brings great glory to God!

Notice in Matthew 19:9 that Jesus distinguishes between fornication and adultery. The word fornication in this verse comes from the Greek word "porneia." It includes adultery, but indicates a lifestyle and a way of thinking as opposed to a single act. The word most commonly translated "adultery" in the New Testament is the Greek word "moicha," which means a single sexual act with someone other than one's spouse.

The reason for the distinction is that adultery implies a single act, whereas fornication indicates a lifestyle. While adultery offers a Scriptural reason for divorce, the child of God motivated by love should ponder long and hard over divorcing a spouse due to a single act of adultery.

If you are in the midst of a situation where a spouse has been unfaithful to you, it may be unthinkable to be open to reconciliation. You are angry and crushed by your spouse's betrayal, and rightly so. I would suggest to you, however, that reconciling the marriage may be preferable to a divorce – not only for the married couple involved, but also for any children you have together. God can miraculously heal your marriage of any problem you and your spouse may have, just as He can supernaturally remove cancer from your body. If you are both willing to submit to each other for the sake of your marriage, it *will* be healed in Jesus' name!

Of course, on many occasions only one spouse is willing to continue in the marriage. Abandonment and adultery are inherently selfish acts, and often they are an outward symptom of inward rebellion against God. You may be the collateral damage of your spouse's rebellion, finding yourself in the midst of divorce proceedings whether you want to be or not.

If you are the "innocent spouse" in such a situation – if your wife has abandoned the family, or if your husband is guilty of a lifestyle of fornication – beginning a new relationship may be the last thing on your mind right now. Biblically, however, just as you have the right to a divorce, you have the right to remarry.

Opinions among evangelical leaders vary widely on this issue. Some respected pastors and Bible teachers will only marry couples who have never been divorced. Others will marry couples who have been married any number of times before, even when those divorces do not meet the plain Scriptural tests I have described above. My understanding of the Word of God, however, leads me to conclude that when God has explicitly permitted divorce, he also permits remarriage.

Not everyone who experiences divorce will or should remarry. But many Christians who seek after the will of God for their lives in the aftermath of divorce will find God leading them to a subsequent marriage.

Divorce is always a heart-rending experience for a Christian. It can take as much of a toll on a man or woman emotionally as a heart attack can in the physical sense – and the recovery period can take even longer. In a sense, the tearing apart of what God decrees to be "one flesh" never fully heals, because when a marriage is torn asunder both partners leave parts of themselves behind. It is a time of suffering. But the Bible is full of examples that teach us that to fully appreciate what God has for each of us, it is necessary for us to suffer in some way.

I have ministered to enough divorced people to know that they suffer with the decision, even when they are biblically justified in seeking the divorce. I also know that there is healing and wholeness on the other side of that dark experience. Sometimes the good shines brighter than ever when contrasted with the darkness. Dr. James Dobson uses an excellent word picture that applies here – when you are in a canoe going through the rapids, it's easy to believe that what's on the other side of those rapids is a waterfall! But there is calm water on the other side of the rough passage you may be in right now, even if you can't perceive it.

By the account of everyone I have ever met who has experienced it, divorce is the very definition of "the darkness." But it need not defeat you, and by His power and grace it will not! If you are serious about seeking God's will in the midst of your divorce, you can and will survive the breakup of your marriage. While it is not always advisable for Christians to remarry after a divorce, I have also joyfully borne witness to occasions where remarriage has created a new family that glorifies God and satisfies its members in ways neither partner dreamed possible.

I should note here that in the case of the death of a spouse, the Bible specifically permits remarriage of the surviving believer to another believer. The apostle Paul wrote,

So then if, while her husband liveth, she be married to another man, she shall be called an adulteress: but if her husband be dead, she is free from that law; so that she is no adulteress, though she be married to another man.

–Romans 7:3

In another context, Paul wrote,

I say therefore to the unmarried and widows, It is good for them if they abide even as I [unmarried]. But if they cannot contain, let them marry: for it is better to marry than to burn.

–1 Corinthians 7:8,9

There is one other situation where I believe that remarriage after a divorce is permissible: when the divorce occurs before the divorced person is born again and filled with the Holy Ghost. I am convinced this is true because I believe in the truth of Paul's declaration that *"if any man be in Christ, he is a new creature: old things are passed away; behold, all things are become new" (2 Corinthians 5:17)*. Because we know that God gives us a clean slate when we exchange our lives for His, we can be assured that our transgressions are forgiven before Him – even if those transgressions include a divorce and remarriage that would otherwise be biblically forbidden. Of course, the legal and moral consequences of your previous marriage – financial obligations, children and so on – remain your responsibility in the new marriage.

Thriving Once Put Asunder

A second marriage, especially one that results in a blended family, provides special challenges for every family member. Here's how to overcome them:

Follow the Rules. The biblical standards I have discussed previously in this book are crucial for any family, but especially one in which either the husband or wife have been previously married. To these families, I say – deviate from God's design for marriage at your peril. Heartache awaits you if you allow any other standard for behavior to creep into your lives.

For example, I have dealt with couples in which one partner or the other will not fully submit to his or her spouse, because of their memories of a previous relationship. In their flesh, a husband cannot trust his new wife to handle the family finances, because his former wife was a compulsive shopper, and a wife makes it difficult for her new husband to travel on business because of her former husband's fornication.

To such couples I say: the biblical rules that bind husbands and wives are even more important for you than for fresh-scrubbed couples just embarking on their first marriage! You know the cost of being out of the will of God where your marriage is concerned; don't doom your new marriage to failure because you cannot bring yourself to obey Him.

Keep the Marriage Primary. A second marriage, especially one with children from previous relationships, is fragile. Pressures come from the children themselves, from former spouses and from current and former in-laws. It's enough to make husband and wife forget why they wanted to get married in the first place. So don't forget! Nurture that marriage as though it was the bedrock foundation of the entire family – because it is.

Focus on keeping the marriage solid. Make sure it the strongest relationship in the new family. All other relationships, even between parents and their biological children, are no less important, but must be subordinate to the marriage. A marriage in which one of the partners continually challenges the other not to "come between me and *my* kids" is one that is headed for trouble.

Nurture the New Family Unit. Even though a blended family has a new marriage at its core, it's important to remember that a host of other new relationships are beginning. Like any relationship, bonds between parents and children, as well as between stepparents and stepchildren, have to be established and maintained, and that takes time. Be sure to make time for each new relationship in the family.

Wives, this may mean you'll have to allow your new husband to take your son to breakfast on a Saturday morning for some "guy time." Husbands, you may need to let your new wife take your daughters shopping for school clothes. Both of you may need to tell your parents that their time with the grandchildren will need to be sharply curtailed while your new family is building a solid relational foundation.

Your children will be affected by the need to establish new relationships as well. Teenagers especially may resent losing time with their friends when a new family is formed. Developing any relationship requires a sacrifice of time and emotional energy. Taking short cuts to relationship building simply won't do – and that's especially true with a blended family.

Budget Carefully and Cautiously. Most second marriages face financial pressures, in the form of alimony and child support, other families simply don't have to deal with. The best way to handle this is for the husband and wife to communicate regularly about upcoming expenses.

In hectic blended families, the temptation is especially great to salve an absent parent's guilty conscience by making extravagant purchases for a child that doesn't live with one of his parents anymore. This should be avoided at all costs. However, husbands and fathers must not shrink from their legal financial obligations that originate from a previous marriage. Paul wrote, *"But if any provide not for his own, and specially for those of his own house, he hath denied the faith, and is worse than an infidel" (1 Timothy 5:8).*

Respect the Baggage. A favorite song, the smell of a particular dish cooking in the kitchen, a Christmas decoration or just the mention of a person's name can stir up painful memories that we thought we had dealt with. These reminders of a painful earlier marriage can ambush you at any time, without warning or consideration, even after you were sure you had dealt with the feelings they recall.

If you've been divorced, you have this kind of emotional baggage. So does your new spouse. You can't avoid it. You can, however, choose to minimize the impact the baggage of your previous marriage has on your new one. One way to do this is to intentionally start new family traditions that have no connection at all to established traditions of any other family member. You may decide, for example, to schedule an annual Christmas-season shopping trip for Mom and her stepchildren to buy something special for Dad. Or you may go somewhere on vacation that nobody in the family has been to before.

The key is to establish the blended family as a distinct unit, with its own traditions and customs. It should never become the new and improved version of either the mother's or the father's previous family.

Above all, make Christ and His Church the center of your new family's existence. Bring your children and stepchildren to church, and become part of the church family.

Notes

Chapter One: Families by the Book

1. Chris Columbus, Director, *Mrs. Doubtfire*, 1993.

Chapter Four: Families by the Book

1. The Barna Group, 1957 Ventura, CA, 93003. www.barna.org Barna Update, September 8, 2004, "Born Again Christians Just As Likely to Divorce As Are Non-Christians," (Accessed December 8, 2006). Used by permission.
2. Ibid.
3. DivorceCare is an excellent, Christ-centered program many churches offer for men and women who are separated or divorced. Their website, www.divorcecare.com, includes more information and a directory of churches that offer the program.

About the Author

ROD PARSLEY, bestselling author of more than sixty books, is the dynamic pastor of World Harvest Church in Columbus, Ohio, a church with ten worldwide ministries and a global outreach. As a highly sought-after crusade and conference speaker whom God has raised up as a prophetic voice to America and the world, Parsley is calling people to Jesus Christ through the good news of the Gospel.

He oversees Bridge of Hope Missions, Harvest Preparatory School, World Harvest Bible College, and the *Breakthrough* broadcast, a television and radio show seen by millions and broadcast to nearly 200 countries around the world, including a potential viewing audience of 97% of the homes in the United States and 78% in Canada. *Breakthrough* is carried on 1,400 stations and cable affiliates, including the Trinity Broadcasting Network, the Canadian Vision Network, Armed Forces Radio and Television Network, and in several countries spanning the globe. In addition, Parsley works as an integral part of other worldwide ministry outreaches and serves on the board of several local and international organizations.

Parsley's refreshingly direct style encourages Christians to examine and eradicate sin from their lives. A fearless champion of living God's way, Parsley follows the high standard set by Jesus Christ and compels his readers to do the same. He and his wife Joni have two children, Ashton and Austin.

OTHER BOOKS BY ROD PARSLEY

Ancient Wells, Living Water

At the Cross, Where Healing Begins

Could It Be?

The Days Before Eternity

He Came First

It's Already There

No Dry Season (Bestseller)

No More Crumbs (Bestseller)

On the Brink (Bestseller)

Repairers of the Breach

Silent No More (#1 Bestseller)

For more information about *Breakthrough*,
World Harvest Church, World Harvest Bible College,
Harvest Preparatory School, The Center for Moral Clarity, or
to receive a product list of the many books, CDs, and DVDs
by Rod Parsley, write or call:

BREAKTHROUGH/WORLD HARVEST CHURCH
P.O. Box 32932
Columbus, OH 43232-0932 USA
(614) 837-1990 (Office)
www.breakthrough.net

WORLD HARVEST BIBLE COLLEGE
P.O. Box 32901
Columbus, OH 43232-0901 USA
(614) 837-4088
www.worldharvestbiblecollege.org

HARVEST PREPARATORY SCHOOL
P.O. Box 32903
Columbus, OH 43232-0903 USA
(614) 837-1990
www.harvestprep.org

THE CENTER FOR MORAL CLARITY
P.O. Box 32903
Columbus, OH 43232-9926 USA
(614) 382-1188
www.CenterForMoralClarity.net

If you need prayer, Breakthrough Prayer Warriors are ready
to pray with you 24 hours a day, 7 days a week at
(800) 424-8644.